52 Kids who R.O.C.K. Every Day

Inspiring stories from young people who Radiate Outrageous Compassion & Kindness

with tips for Acts of Kindness & Service Projects PLUS 21 Day Reflection Journal

Kim David
with Stella David

Project Stella Resources

A simple act of caring creates an endless ripple that comes back to you.

- Multiple sources

This Book belongs to:

_____

PURPOSE OF THIS BOOK

The purpose of this book is to **inspire kids** from all around the world **to transform** their homes, schools, and communities because they Radiate Outrageous Compassion & Kindness.

Through this book we will **change the world** by sharing inspiring stories, giving really great tips, and guiding YOU to do your own acts of kindness.

Why is it important for kids my age to be kind and compassionate to others?

"It's important to be kind to others because when you are kind to them, they'll be kind to someone else, who'll be kind to someone else, and so on..."

– Adelia, age 7.

Have you ever done something kind for someone because someone else did something kind for you? How did it make you feel?

_____

_____

_____

_____

Meet ANGELA

Age 7

Why is it important for kids my age to be kind and compassionate to others?

"Being kind and compassionate is important because you help others, and being kind is the right thing to do and how you should always be."

At Angela's school, there is a buddy bench. If a child has no one to play with, they can sit on the bench until someone will play with him or her. Angela will watch the buddy bench at all times while she's playing just to make sure that if there's anyone who sits on it, she can get them off it by playing with them.

If someone is mean to someone else, Angela will make sure she speaks up and tries to resolve issues for others. Angela also cares deeply about animals. She had found a bird that couldn't fly and she insisted that it was brought somewhere to get it help.

R.O.C.K. with this Project
Create a "Buddy" Bench for your School

Supplies Needed

- Designated Picnic Table or Bench
- Paint
- Inspiring Quote
- Sharpies

Steps for Project

You could purchase a "Buddy" Bench for your school (ask a parent to search online) or you could make one.

Talk to the Principal or Director of your school and let them know why you think one is needed.

Ask if a picnic table or bench on the playground can be designated.

Paint it a bright color or make it look really cheerful. Students can then write positive messages or quotes on the bench.

Have everyone sign the bench to show they support it.

Then, when someone is feeling lonely and would like someone to play with – they can sit on the bench. Then everyone knows to invite him or her to come and play!

Meet ANNE

Age 11

Why is it important for kids my age to be kind and compassionate to others?

"It is important for kids my age to be kind and compassionate to others because, we all have to share this planet together and we should help each other out instead of hurting each other. One little act of kindness can effect many people in a good way."

Anne wants to go to Disney herself but her family is not able to take her right now. She has a chance to earn a trip to Disney by selling 5000 boxes of Girl Scout cookies. She has the goal to sell 5000 boxes but plans to give her trip away to another child that is sick. Anne volunteers at a local veteran's home and she reads to kids when she can.

Why is it important for kids my age to be kind and compassionate to others?

"Because if you're not kind it's a mean town and everyone is always mad at each other."

- Jake, age 3

Meet ASHTYN
Age 11

Why is it important for kids my age to be kind and compassionate to others?

"It is important to be kind and compassionate to everyone especially at my age for confidence and self esteem as well as to be an example for future generations and those around me!"

Ashtyn has proven to her friends and family that she can be a good citizen and kind and loving to others no matter who they are and where they are from. She has done community service projects through church and school.

Ashtyn won a Citizenship Award because she demonstrates leadership, responsibility and citizenship. She is a young role model for kindness, citizenship, fairness, leadership, responsibility, respect and caring.

R.O.C.K. with this Project
Create Community Displays

Display Supplies

- Poster Board
- Markers
- Color Paper
- Glue, Scissors, Craft supplies
- Books or Printouts for Ideas

Show off what is great about your community and what you appreciate. Make a poster board displays of what you like the most about their community.

Display Ideas

- What is special about our community?

- Where do you like to go in our community?

- Are there people who have helped you out?

- What do you like to do that is close to your school or your home?

Where to Display

*Pick somewhere that gets a good amount of traffic from community members

- Library
- Town Hall
- Community Center
- Recreation Center

Meet BREA

Age 11

Why is it important for kids my age to be kind and compassionate to others?

"Because you want others to treat others the way you would want to be treated."

Brea is kind and compassionate towards people and animals. She wants to make a difference in this world. She doesn't ask for recognition and she always does it from the kindness of her heart. Brea won Student of the Month and her teacher said, "she is respectful and a friend to everyone inside and outside the classroom; she always does the right thing even when no one is watching."

Brea is the President of Student Council and her school collected non-perishable items for a food bank that was recently robbed and for other organizations that fed children, families, and elderly members of the community. Her school filled 3 vans full of can food items!

R.O.C.K. with this Project
Fun Can Food Drive Tips

Canned Food Drive Tip - Create a Recipe Book

Tired of getting the "rejected" canned food items that no one really eats? To encourage that donations are made of more commonly requested items, let your youth know that they will be creating a recipe book based on what is received.

Things you need:

- List of items that are donated or that you want to be donated
- Provide this list to all the youth and have them submit a recipe they find
- Have a small committee responsible for collecting the recipes, typing them in a booklet, and then printing them out.
- Join forces with a community sponsor who could help print the recipe book. You would need enough copies that the food pantry can hand out during a two week period.

Canned Food Drive Tip - Build Structures from Canned Goods

To begin, let students know that they will be collecting nonperishable items but before they are donated they are going to build a structure from the items they collect. Think Grocery Store canned good structures for Football season or for the Holidays.

Things you need:

- A theme – Seven Wonders Around the World, Holiday Celebrations, Patriotic, School Spirit, etc.
- Time to plan – Participants will want to draw out the structure they want to build. Decide if any other supplies are needed to make the structure happen.
- Time to collect items – give the students a week to get donations. There might be specific items they need. Remind everyone that when the structures are completed and judged, all items will be donated to a local food pantry.
- Judges – have three nonpartial judges. They can be from the community. Have someone who represents the food pantry serve as a judge. You can also use Social Media to judge – Post pictures of each structure and see which one gets the most "likes".

Why is it important for kids my age to be kind and compassionate to others?

"So people know that you care and they would want to be your friend."

– Caroline, age 9

Meet CHLOE

Age 7

KIDS WHO R.O.C.K. FINALIST

Why is it important for kids my age to be kind and compassionate to others?

"I think because we NEED to love others! Even if they're not in our family we are all in the same community. God tells me every day, in my heart, to care for others and that's what I'm going to do."

A few years ago Chloe's family made the decision to become a foster home for young children. Chloe was beyond excited to share her home with children in great need of one. She went home and started going through her things to get it ready for a another child to come in. Even through the challenges of opening her home to other kids, Chloe is focused on showing kindness.

"I don't know why kids have to hurt. There are lots of sad things in life. It makes my heart hurt inside but I love them and will help."

R.O.C.K. with this Project

School Supply & Book Drive – plan for January

Supplies Needed

- Box in each hallway for collections
- Fliers to promote
- Brown Grocery Bags to pack kits

You can plan a school supply and book drive to help teachers at your school and other schools (creating unity) in the community.

Supplies to Collect

School supplies are often donated in July and August but when January comes around most have already been used. Most teachers end up using their own money to get supplies for the classroom. This School Supply and Book Drive helps them get ready for the new semester and takes some of that stress away.

- Tissue Boxes
- Cleaning Wipes
- Hand wipes
- Sandwich, Quart or Gallon Baggies
- Paper towels
- Dry Erase Markers
- Number 2 Pencils (write encouraging messages on them with sharpies)
- Pink erasers
- Permanent markers
- Fun stickers
- Individually packaged snacks - some teachers purchase snacks for children that come to school hungry

Why is it important for kids my age to be kind and compassionate to others?

"*Cause if you're not kind you won't end up with many friends and if you ever had friends they won't respect you as much.*"

– Roz, age 8

Meet CREATING HOPE CLUB

Started with 10 Members

This middle school group started because they wanted to create hope for the students at their school that felt bad about themselves. They talked about there needing to be a change, so the club decided to be the change.

10 students grew to 21 students as they completed projects that spread kindness to everyone. And in helping others feel good, they noticed they felt better also. Their favorite act of kindness is writing positive notes and making sure everyone at the school gets one.

R.O.C.K. with this Project
Start A Kindness Club

A Kindness Club can transform your school. It encourages and inspires students to think beyond themselves and seek out opportunities to show compassion and kindness.

By creating a Kindness Club for your school, you are making it public that kindness and compassion is something valued. It doesn't take a lot of talent or skill to participate in kindness activities so it is something that is inclusive to everyone. With administrative support it can be made as important as any sports team or theater program. AND you don't have to worry about a losing season. Kindness always wins.

Anyone can be part of the Kindness Club and they can all feel good about what is being done. Valuable skills are developed and it gives a great thing to talk about on college applications and in job interviews.

Students of all abilities can feel like they are doing their best in a Kindness Club. It can quickly become your largest club on your campus.

It does not cost much to start! You don't need special equipment. Students don't need to by a uniform or musical instrument. You can start out with an Advisor, 3-4 students, some construction paper, and markers.

Your first act of kindness can be your recruitment tool. How great is this! The main resources you need is a little time and students with a positive attitude.

Meet THE DIVERSITY CLUB

Beatrix, Emily, Lilly, Tuala, Sophia, and Mary Rose

This Middle School Club with 12 members created a "Start with a Hello" Week at their school to encourage kindness and stop bullying.

The members in the club planned activities to encourage students to include everyone in feeling part of the community and welcomed at their school.

Activities they planned

- A photo booth with fun, silly props
- A "Hello" day where everyone wore name tags and were encouraged to say hello to as many people as they could
- A sticky note banner with positive messages
- A day where bookmarks were placed on every locker
- A celebration of Acts of Kindness where members of the club gave out lollipops to anyone they caught in the act.

GLOBAL YOUTH SERVICE DAY CELEBRATION

SIMPLE PROJECTS, MAJOR IMPACT

R.O.C.K. with the Project

STUDENTS WILL TAKE PART IN FOUR SERVICE PROJECT STATIONS THAT EACH ADDRESS A DIFFERENT ISSUE

ANIMALS

MAKE DOG & CAT TOYS

Tie fabric and stuff t-shirts with soft materials to create toys and pillows for animal shelter

MAKE A CHEMO CARE KIT FOR KIDS

HEALTH

Comfort Kits include
- Items that help with side effects
- Comfort item
-Activity item

SENIORS

MAKE NON SLIP SOCKS FOR NURSING HOME

Students use puffy paint to create designs (dots, circles, zig zags) on the bottom of socks

MAKE A CARD TO GO IN A TROOP CARE KIT

VETERANS

Students make cards and pick one item from table to go in a Troop Care Package to be sent from the School

Meet EMILY

Age 10

Why is it important for kids my age to be kind and compassionate to others?

"To make people smile"

Emily supported her little sister at a very difficult time of their lives. RayRay, her little sister, was diagnosed with a type of cancer. RayRay went through treatment, a very harsh treatment for two years. Emily has been a GREAT big sister to be by her side and never complain. Emily visited one of RayRay's clinic appointments to see what her sister had to go through, she was sad to see the kids being poked and sick. She decided she wanted to put smiles on their face with toys.

Emily developed a non profit organization named, **Ray's Your Hair**. Emily and her sister deliver toys to children waiting at the clinic or have an extended hospital stay.

Why is it important for kids my age to be kind and compassionate to others?

"Cause if you are mean to them it lives with them for the rest of their lives and that's not something people need to live with. "

– Jenna, age 12

Meet GARRETT

Age 11

Garrett was taught to knit by his grandmother. He used the skill to help keep him calm since he is always full of energy.

Then after his friend was diagnosed with cancer, Garrett decided to use what he was taught to help others. He now knits hats for children with cancer and donates them to the hospital. He says that it is meeting other kids who were doing service that inspired him to do more.

Meet Austin

Austin learned that some kids didn't have winter hats and gloves. So, he decided he wanted to help by collecting the things that they need. He and his mom started Austin's Closet so that children could get the items from donations and community support.

R.O.C.K. with this Project
Coat & Scarf Drive
for People who are Currently Homeless

Coat Drive Supplies

- Big Box located in the front office
- Fliers to publicize
- Fleece materials to make scarfs
- Fabric marker

You can collect coats from home and ask your neighbors to assist.

Coats of all sizes are needed.

You can also cut Fleece material to make scarves to attach with each coat.

How to Make a No-sew Fleece Scarf

Step One
Trim the Edges to make fabric even

Step Two
Cut Fringes- 1/2 wide strips about 4 inches into the ends of the scarf.

Step 3 – Tie (Optional)
Wrap one fringe around your finger to the right, bring around back coming forward on your left then tuck the end down thru the loop you just made and pull gently.

Meet HARRISON

High School Senior

At 12 years old, Harrison felt different because he had a lot of energy but didn't know what to do with it. Then, he found that his interest in BMX let him focus that energy so he could be successful.

Harrison decided that he could help other kids. He started a group called "Gear Up" and helps kids feel good about themselves by getting them on bikes and having mentors to help them succeed.

Meet ALEX

Age 10

Alex was beaten up because other kids thought he was different. Alex decided that no other kid should every feel bad about being a "nerd" so he decided to make it something fun and celebrated.

Alex created a project called "Build a Bow for a Purpose". The project teaches other kids about positive self-image and that each person is special.

Why is it important for kids my age to be kind and compassionate to others?

"...so they don't get mad."

– Will, age 4

"...because you should not be rude to anyone."

- Jax, age 7

Meet HOLLY

Age 17

"Imagine how amazing the world would be if everyone was kind and compassionate to each other and put others needs above their own? One person can't impact the world but you can make a world of difference for a person you help! Let's all do our part by actively looking to make a difference every single day!"

Holly is selfless, compassionate, and is always putting others above herself. Her first desire is to give and never hesitates to jump in and help someone in need. She is a leader in the community and is well known as a hard working and dedicated teenager. She was chosen as a finalist for the Philanthropy Tank where she pitched her plan to provide free horseback riding programs for inner city youth and was awarded a $14,000 grant for **Horses That Help** to purchase a new horse trailer for the program. She earned so many hours for her volunteer work that she was honored with the Presidential "Spirit of Community" award this past year!

R.O.C.K. with this Project
Appreciation Bags for First Responders

Supplies Needed

- Paper Lunch Bags
- Color paper for making cards
- Crayons/Markers

Donated items

- Small bottles of water
- Instant Coffee pouches
- Individual bags of snacks
- Gum
- Tissues
- Band-Aids
- Car Freshener
- Pocket-size book of Inspirational Sayings

Show your appreciation to First Responders by creating bags for them to use while they are on the job.

Hold a donation drive to have families provide items listed on the supplies.

Students make personal cards to be included in the bags and they can decorate the bags.

Once bags are completed deliver them to your local police and fire stations.

Meet JARED, SAMANTHA, & ANDREW

High School Students

Not wanting kids who are homeless to not get to celebrate their birthdays, these three friends created an organization called "B.Box".

With their motto, "Celebrate. Smile. Repeat.", they were able to collect donations to put together boxes that included everything a child might need to celebrate a birthday.

These birthday boxes are taken to local youth shelters and a celebration happens with cake, candles, balloons, and decorations.

Even if the party doesn't happen on the child's or teen's actual birth date, they are able to feel important by having someone that cares celebrate with them.

R.O.C.K. with this Project

Collect Blankets & Toiletry Kits for Victims of Human Trafficking

Supplies Needed

* Donation boxes for each hall
* Fliers asking for donations
* Gallon size Plastic Baggies

Human Trafficking is the modern day form of slavery. Survivors of Human Trafficking often stay in shelters until safe homes are found.

Steps:

Step 1: Ask students to donate new or gently used blankets

Step 2: Have a volunteer wash all the gently used blankets

Step 3: Assemble Toiletry kits by putting soap, toothpaste, shampoo, deodorant, wash cloth, hand wipes, etc. in the gallon size bag.

Make your Own Blankets to Donate

Supplies Needed

* Fleece material of similar sizes
* Scissors

Step 1: Choose the Fabric. Choose a print and a contrasting or matching solid.

Step 2: Line Up the Two Fabric Pieces.

Step 3: Trim to the Same Size.

Step 4: Cut Out the Corners.

Step 5: Cutting the Fringe.

Step 6: Begin Tying Knots. And continue Around the Blanket.

Meet JASMINE
Age 16

"It is important for kids my age to be kind and compassionate about others because some people are less fortunate. Most kids my age do not understand that they are blessed to have the opportunities that they have now. Kids my age should learn to care about others and the importance of helping others. People who do not have the amazing advantages I have suffer from extreme lost of hope. I believe that the world should be a happier place for everyone without all the struggling some people have to go through. This is why I strongly support community service. Giving back to the community makes you feel like you are helping the world little by little. Kids my age should learn to accept the fact that they are grateful and be more considerate of others because they need to understand that they could be the one who is less fortunate. If kids my age learned to place themselves in someone else's shoes they would know how much love it would mean to others to be kind."

Jasmine seeks ways to better her community both in 4-H and outside of 4-H. Jasmine always puts others before herself and she loves with a big heart. Jasmine leads a community service club each summer and received the outstanding community service project award for Northwest District through 4-H. She is kind and welcoming and sees the good in everyone.

R.O.C.K. with this Project

Plants for Veterans

Supplies Needed

- Plastic Flower Pots
- Soil
- Flowers
- Sharpies to decorate the pot
- Colored paper to make cards

Planning the Project

Brighten up a Veteran's day by presenting him or her with a plant to beautify their home or work and to give something small to care for.

Decorate the plastic flower pots with sharpies, paint pens, and stickers. Take flowers to place in pot and fill the rest with soil. There are many local organizations for Veterans that the pots can be donated to and if there is a Veteran's Appreciation Ceremony taking place, the pots can be given as gifts.

Make the gift more special by including handwritten encouragement notes or drawings.

Meet JOSEPH

Age 19

Wanting to bring Christmas to children receiving treatment at a local Children's Hospital, Joseph raised money through GoFundMe to purchase Christmas Trees for over 50 kids.

He organized young volunteers to set-up the trees so the children that are sick and their families could enjoy.

Meet the "HOLIDAY HERO" Sisters

Two sisters in Georgia sold hot chocolate and set up a GoFundMe page to raise money to purchase Christmas gifts and groceries for three families in need. They were able to partner with a local fast food restaurant to sell their hot chocolate outside the store and talk to people about how they were helping families.

5 GIFT GIVING IDEAS TO ENCOURAGE KINDNESS FROM KIDS THIS HOLIDAY SEASON

Incorporate ONE of these ideas in your gift-giving tradition this year

R.O.C.K. with this Project

ADOPT-A-FAMILY

BUDGET TO TAKE YOUR CHILDREN SHOPPING TO PURCHASE GIFTS FOR CHILDREN THEIR SAME AGE

GIFT EXPECTATIONS

DISCUSS WITH YOUR KIDS THAT THEY WILL EACH RECEIVE

A WANT, A NEED, A WEAR, A READ & A GIFT TO DO A GOOD DEED

PAY IT FORWARD:

FOR EVERY GIFT THEY RECEIVE - ENCOURAGE YOUR CHILD TO DONATE AN ITEM THEY NO LONGER USE

WHITE ENVELOPE TRADITION

HONOR A FAMILY MEMBER BY GIVING A GIFT TO A COMMUNITY ORGANIZATION HE OR SHE SUPPORTED

DO AN ANIMAL GIFT

CHECK OUT HEIFER INTERNATIONAL AND SAMARITAN'S PURSE FOR OPTIONS TO GIFT COWS, CHICKS, AND GOATS THAT BENEFIT OTHER COUNTRIES

Why is it important for kids my age to be kind and compassionate to others?

"Kids have to be kind because they make grownups be kind. Whenever I'm happy - you are happy - but when I am bad, you get mad. Kind kids means kind moms"

— Kendall, age 5

When you are kind to others, how do they respond? When you are kind to someone else, are they kind back?

_____

_____

_____

_____

Meet KASEY

Age 11

Kasey has been bullied for many years. She has attended 3 different schools, trying to escape the cruelty that comes from being different.

Kasey had to go to the hospital and the day after Kasey returned home from the hospital, she went with her mom to the grocery store. The woman ahead of her dropped something while loading her groceries onto the conveyor belt. Despite being sad and not feeling well, Kasey picked the item up, put it on the belt, and smiled at the woman. At the library, she held the door open for several people, even though temperatures were well below freezing.

Her kind gestures are automatic, like breathing. She can no more give up kindness than she can give up inhaling and exhaling.

Meet KATIE

Age 19

At age 9, Katie took care of a cabbage plant until it grew to be 40 lbs! She donated her cabbage to a soup kitchen to feed people in need. She then started a garden to be able to feed more people with the vegetables she donated.

Katie's project turned into an organization called **Katie's Krops**. There are more than 100 gardens helping feed people through the program.

Meet TUCKER & ADDIE

Tucker and Addie are brother and sister. They volunteer with other kids to glean. Gleaning is a process where you go to a garden, farm, or orchard and pick up the produce that has fallen or no one wants. While the food might not look pretty it can still be used. The Society of St. Andrew have families volunteer to glean and the food is donated to help feed others.

Why is it important for kids my age to be kind and compassionate to others?

"So when we grow up we know what it means to be kind to others and we do it more often".

– Ricky, age 11

Meet KYLE
Age 16

Why is it important for kids my age to be kind and compassionate to others?

"Because it effects them physically and mentally. And the most important thing to do right now is to be nice to people."

Kyle is hardworking, smart, kind, amazing, talented, caring, strong and everything in between. He constantly wants to help others before himself. He's stubborn in the way he doesn't want anyone to help him because he wants to help them.

What is something that makes you really sad or mad? What can you do to make the situation better for someone?

_____

_____

_____

_____

R.O.C.K. with this Project

Record Kids Reading for Nursing Homes or Cancer Treatment Centers

Supplies Needed

- Books
- Recording Device
- Art supplies to make cards

Planning the Project

This is a great project to help kids practice their reading and to provide something for Veterans undergoing medical treatment to listen to. This project was first completed for cancer patients having chemotherapy.

You will need some recording device. Could be with a tablet and computer or could be a classroom listening center and lecture recording.

But the final product needs to be in a format that patients can have access to listen to.

Meet LEXI

Age 17

Music is very important to Lexi and she knows it is important to other students at her school and in her community. But when her community stopped having an event to showcase the musical talents of all the students, Lexi knew she needed to provide a away for them to still be recognized for their passion.

Lexi organized an Extravaganza to let musical groups show off and know their performances are just important at sports. She also made sure that she had activities for the whole family to keep everyone excited and entertained.

Lexi took something she is interested in and helped other students with the same interest know they are important.

R.O.C.K. with this Project
Poetry Slam & Dessert Fundraiser
Supplies Needed

- List of poems that students can pick from or have them write their own
- Desserts donated by parents and community members
- Tables, Chairs, & Table cloths
- Plates, Napkins, Serving Utensils
- Sound System
- Invitations to Friends, Family, and Special Guests

Part One - Poetry Slam

1. Have students think about a cause or an issue that means a lot to them. You can ask, "What makes you mad, sad or really happy?"

2. Students can write their own poem or find another poem that discusses the issue

3. Students should practice reciting their poem so they can read out loud to friends, family members, and guests

TIP: To help students participate that may not like being in front of a crowd, let them submit artwork and drawings that represent the issue that means a lot to them. Let every voice be heard.

Part Two - Dessert Fundraiser

Turn your event into a Fundraiser to raise money for a community organization that your students vote for.

1. Have desserts donated by family members and school staff.
2. Ask for desserts to be brought early so they can be portioned equally
3. Price desserts - suggested $1 slice of cake/pie, 2 cookies for $1
4. If there is a special dessert made, do a Silent Auction with starting bid $5 or $10
5. Serve Coffee and Lemonade for free beside a Donation Bucket

Why is it important for kids my age to be kind and compassionate to others?

"Show kindness to each other because it can really affect someone's life or even decision to go forward with life"

– Mack, age 15

Meet MADISON

Age 5

Madison was born with some very unique challenges. She goes to physical, occupational, and speech therapies every week. It will be a lifetime of doctor appointments, therapies, and more surgeries.

But even will all the doctors' appointments she is almost always smiling, laughing, dancing, being friendly to everyone she meets. While her physical communication is not the norm, it is her strong spirit that lifts others up. Nobody is as brave as Madison.

Meet MIA

Age 12

Mia's dream is to be a doctor. She has learned about many diseases and enjoys participating in fundraising events that benefit people in need.

Mia has volunteered at the Alzheimer's Association walk and cheered for the walkers. She also volunteered at Lung Association's walk passing out water and cheering. She has volunteered at the Relay for Life two years in a row, along with the Believe Cancer Walk.

Mia has collected food for the food banks and also gathered items needed for the Ronald McDonald House of Charities. She enjoyed making blankets for the kids at the Loma Linda Children's Hospital. Mia can't wait to be old enough to work in a community kitchen to feed the homeless.

R.O.C.K. with this Project

Packaging Meals for Shelters or Foster Homes

Meal Packaging Supplies

- Brown lunch bags (bags with sturdy handles are great because they can be reused)
- Gloves
- Paper towels
- Plastic utensils

You can pack lunch bags to be delivered to local shelters and/or foster homes.

Decorate bags with encouraging messages or uplifting pictures

Suggestions for Bags

*Tip - If you are packing meals for adults that are currently homeless, you want to make sure you pack soft items. Some adults may have sensitive teeth and have a hard time chewing.

- Hard-boiled Eggs
- Peanut Butter & Jelly Sandwiches
- Bananas
- Cheese sticks
- Packaged crackers - cheese on wheat
- Fruit cups (make sure you include a plastic spoon)
- Bottled Water
- Napkins/Paper Towels

Meet NATE

Age 11

Nate was worried about young babies not having enough to eat when their families did not have enough food. Nate decided to start fundraising to get money for his "Baby Food Fund."

Nate plans food drives to collect baby food and partners with his local food bank so the food can get to the families with infants.

Meet JORDAN

Age 10

At a very young age Jordan was able to take an interest he had in architecture to create a wonderful way to help people who do not have homes and not always able to get to a shelter.

Jordan designed a tent that can provide temporary housing and he created easy to move furniture so that kids would have a desk to use – no matter where they had to sleep at night.

R.O.C.K. with this Project

Disaster Preparedness Kits

Supplies Needed

- Plastic tubs with lids
- Blank form to write Emergency numbers

Donations to Collect

- First aid supplies
- Bottled water
- Nonperishable foods
- Manual can openers (Dollar Store)
- Flashlights
- Batteries

Planning the Project

Hold a donation drive for ask for project sponsors to provide items listed above.

Students will fill plastic tubs with emergency preparedness supplies and also learn about who to contact when an emergency happens. They can start filling out the "Who to Contact" form together but finish at home with their parents.

Spread the impact by donating the kits to families and elderly in the community.

Meet RACHEL

Age 9

Why is it important for kids my age to be kind and compassionate to others?

"It's important to help the environment, because it's the only one that we have. And it's important to help others and be kind, because that is how we would want other people to treat us. If everyone was kind and compassionate – the world would be a much better place."

Rachel decided that too many crayons end up in the landfills every year. So, she helped create a flyer that got sent out to families and she collected used and broken crayons that people were going to throw away. Over the summer she sorted them and recycled all of the broken, useless pieces.

The crayons that she saved from the landfill were new or like new and she has been distributing those to the zoo, area daycares, and to local children's hospitals.

R.O.C.K. with this Project
"Thank You" Placemats for Firefighters

Supplies Needed

- Legal Size Paper or Construction paper
- Patriotic Coloring pages
- Crayons/Markers
- Lamination or Clear Contact Paper

Planning the Project

Firefighters work several days in a row without going home. They share their meals in the Firehouse. You can create placemats for the Firefighters to use to remind them each day how thankful we are for the service they provide.

Print out coloring pages or draw your own pictures and messages. Laminate the place mats or cover with clear contact paper.

Deliver your place mats to your local fire station. To increase your impact, include some groceries or homemade goodies.

Meet RILEY

Age 10

Why is it important for kids my age to be kind and compassionate to others?

"It's important for kids my age to be kind and compassionate to others because it makes other people feel good about themselves."

Riley loves animals. She is an artist and an actor. She is working on her Bronze Award for Girl Scouts, which means she has to make the world a better place and she is doing that by keeping things out of the landfills.

When she commits to something, she gives it her all. She just started a dog sitting company and goes above and beyond... walking, feeding, playing, cuddling with each dog.

Meet SOPHIA, MADALENA, & ARIELLA

These three sisters show that doing acts of kindness is a very positive experience when you do it as a family.

Together they have performed numerous acts of kindness in their community, impacting seniors, children, and those who are without food.

Together they have

- Made 1,000 PB&J sandwiches & 55,000 Cookies for people who are experiencing homelessness
- Made 2,000 Easter Baskets for kids and teens in need.
- Sorted supplies to fill 600 Backpacks
- Laid Wreathes of Remembrance for over 7 Years for 2700 veterans
- Donated 1,200 lbs. of Halloween Candy

R.O.C.K. with this Project

PinWheel Project in Remembrance –
September 11

Supplies Needed

- Pinwheels: Flag Pattern or solid Red, White and Blue
- Soft ground outside to place
- Banner Paper and Markers/Paint to make a sign

Planning the Project

Nearly 3,000 people (2,996 according to Wikipedia) died in the attacks on September 11, 2001.

Students can create a display to remember the victims with PinWheels.

It might be difficult and expensive to make or purchase 3,000 Pinwheels. Instead, make a sign explaining what the display is for and say 1 Pinwheel = 10 victims for 300 Pinwheels or 1 Pinwheel = 50 victims for 60 Pinwheels. You can decide based on the number of volunteers that can help and the number of Pinwheels you have available.

Take the Pinwheels and place outside, sticking them in soft ground or lining the edge of a sidewalk.

Meet
STELLA & KELLY

KIDS WHO R.O.C.K. FINALIST

4th Grade

When trying to decide what they wanted to do for the Bronze Award with Girl Scouts, Stella & Kelly heard about a family that lost their home in a fire. Everything was gone.

They decided that they would help children in crisis and children in Foster Care by making comfort kits. They stuffed reusable bags with school supplies, books, and toiletries.

They also held an event for kids in their community to come and hand stuffed 150 animals. These stuffed animals provide a comfort item and are put in the bags for the kids who need them.

Meet TY

Age 11

Why is it important for kids my age to be kind and compassionate to others?

"If we weren't kind to each other, the world would be a really bad place. We need kindness to lift each other up. It is important to serve people because it is the right thing to do."

Ty is a true kind-hearted leader. He always finds a way to make everyone feel special. He seeks out the underdog and always includes them and boost their self-worth by showing them their strengths. He loves sports. He loves to boost the morale of his team. Even when he's not on the field he's cheering on those who are. He understands the value of each person in his school and in his community and he make sure that they understand that they are valued as well.

Why is it important for kids my age to be kind and compassionate to others?

"It's important for kids my age to be compassionate and kind to others so they can be an example to others."

- Thiery, age 8

Meet VICTOR

Age 5

Each February there is a special day that people are encouraged to do Random Acts of Kindness for total strangers. Victor was caught doing this at a local restaurant where he went to people he did not know and handed out coupons for free custard.

He was able to get the coupons by saving them for months from his kid's meals. This is just one way of many that Victor has inspired community members for a year to spread kindness around.

Meet a "SECRET ADMIRER"

One "Secret Admirer" felt it was important that everyone at a high school felt appreciated for Valentine's Day. Over 1500 handmade Valentine's Day cards were placed on the lockers of students with the message, "You are loved."

Meet XANDER

Age 10

Why is it important for kids my age to be kind and compassionate to others?

"You should be kind to others because otherwise you could hurt their feelings, and you wouldn't want your feelings to be hurt."

When Xander sees people in need he is the first one to donate or give it to them.

When he turned 9 he had a birthday party where he did not ask for gifts for himself. Instead, he asked for donations for families in need. He donated two vans full of items and gift cards to The House of Refuge.

Fundraising Tips to R.O.C.K.

Ask for Donations

Share your vision with friends and family

Talk about your project. Tell them your vision and what problem you are trying to solve. Be open about what you need. Ask for their support.

Make and Share a Video

Make a video where you talk about your project and also show pictures of people in action. Include a link for your audience to donate. Ask them to share your video.

Set up a Social Media Fundraiser

Facebook now allows you to set up a fundraiser for your friends to donate online. Create a donation page with information about your project and a deadline.

Fundraising Tips to R.O.C.K.

Sell Something

Old Fashion Lemonade Stand

There is a youth movement to have "LemonAid" stands and Bake Sales. Set up a stand for youth to sell and serve homemade goods. Share with your neighbors.

Sell a Craft

Loom Band Bracelets are just one type of craft that is easy for youth to make and sell. Do school colors or the colors for your cause (i.e. pink for Breast Cancer).

Make Inspirational Art

Purchase canvas from the Dollar Store and use sharpies or paint to write inspiring quotes.

Pinterest is your friend!

Fundraising Tips to R.O.C.K.

Apply for Grants

Local Grants

In your community there may be local companies that offer grants. We applied for one through our local EMC. The grant may provide money but it also might need to be used to purchase an item. We used our local grant to purchase a laptop for our brand new service organization.

Matching Grants

Big chain stores might offer matching grants . This means you let them know how much you raised or contributed to the project and they match it up to a certain amount. Some stores require that your project helps a specific issue - so do your research!

National Grants

Youth Service America provides a list of grants and requirements year round. Grants are available for providing projects on certain days or for tackling certain issues. Check out ysa.org for more information.

Fundraising Tips to R.O.C.K.

Sponsorships

Recognize them on a T-shirt

Sponsorships are great because they help you fund your project AND the business or person gets recognition and publicity. I love listing sponsors on the back of a t-shirt because people wear them around and it keeps the sponsors visible.

Sponsorship Levels

By giving options for different sponsorship levels (silver, gold, diamond) you create a bit of competition but you also allow choices. Individuals and small businesses tend to respond better when there is a level meant for them.

In-Kind Sponsorships

Sometimes a business wants to support you but cannot provide you with money. Instead, they might be able to do an In-Kind Sponsorship by providing supplies you need. It might be providing a meal for your volunteers or even a prize you can offer. Think outside the box! You can then use your other donations for other things you need.

Why is it important for kids my age to be kind and compassionate to others?

"It's important to be kind and compassionate to others so that you can make sure they feel good about themselves. It makes them happier and act like better people."

– Zoë, age 11

Describe a time someone showed you kindness. Did your day get better?

_____

_____

_____

_____

Kindness Word Search
Stella David, age 10
Words can be found vertical, horizontal, diagonal, and backwards

A	I	X	W	A	B	U	S	T	E	R	N
E	Y	S	I	L	U	E	L	L	F	G	E
N	C	B	E	Y	L	N	D	I	G	I	N
O	S	A	T	E	L	N	U	O	H	V	D
L	O	W	R	B	Y	Y	H	I	T	I	S
E	E	H	I	I	S	J	O	P	C	N	T
M	K	I	N	D	N	E	S	S	E	G	O
R	M	V	S	N	L	G	H	O	H	V	I
E	W	T	F	K	S	E	R	V	I	C	E
S	O	E	C	R	F	S	E	I	T	B	R
P	Y	O	B	L	H	E	L	P	I	N	G
E	R	O	K	Q	K	I	C	A	L	M	W
C	Z	G	O	I	K	H	M	P	A	L	O
T	S	D	I	K	W	I	A	C	T	S	L

ACTS   BULLY   BUSTER   CARING   GIVING

HELPING   KIDS   KINDNESS   RESPECT   ROCK

SERVICE

Acts of Kindness 21 Day Journal

Questions written with Stella David

How to use this Journal

Part One

Each day there is a question that you can answer. You can draw your answer or write it out. This is your journal so write what you think – it doesn't have to all make sense – just get your thoughts on paper.

Part Two

Use the Kindness Wheel to pick an Act of Kindness to do that day. Color in what you decide to do and then at the end of the day answer the questions.

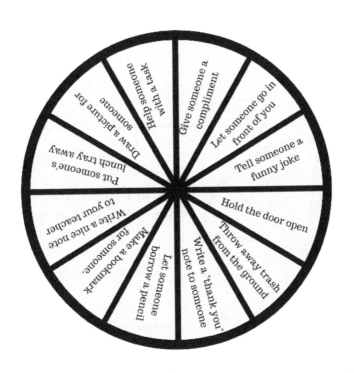

Acts of Kindness Journal

Why is it important for kids your age to be kind and compassionate to others?

Write or draw your answer below.

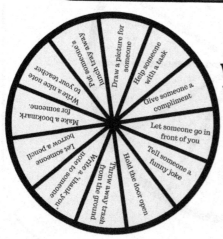

What act of Kindness did you do today? Color it in on the wheel.

Was it easy or hard?

How did it make you feel?

Day Two

Acts of Kindness Journal

What is an example of kindness? What is something you can do to be kind?

Write or draw your answer below.

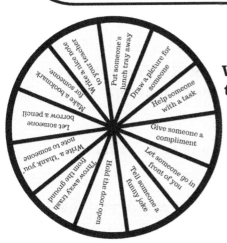

What act of Kindness did you do today? Color it in on the wheel.

Was it easy or hard?

How did it make you feel?

Acts of Kindness Journal

What does compassion mean? How can you be compassionate to someone you know?

Write or draw your answer below.

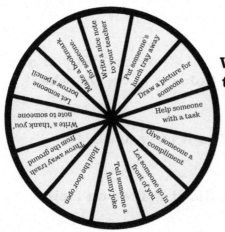

What act of Kindness did you do today? Color it in on the wheel.

Was it easy or hard?

How did it make you feel?

Acts of Kindness Journal

Who is the kindest person you know? What does he or she do that is kind?

Write or draw your answer below.

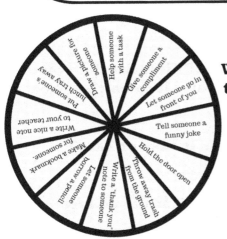

What act of Kindness did you do today? Color it in on the wheel.

Was it easy or hard?

How did it make you feel?

Acts of Kindness Journal

Would you rather... Stand up to a bully with a group of friends or tell the teacher about it?

Write or draw your answer below.

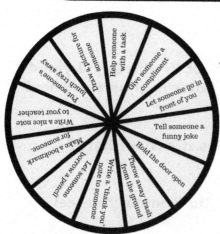

What act of Kindness did you do today? Color it in on the wheel.

Was it easy or hard?

How did it make you feel?

Day Six

Acts of Kindness Journal

Would you rather... get a thank you note or have someone say thank you to you in front of a group?

Write or draw your answer below.

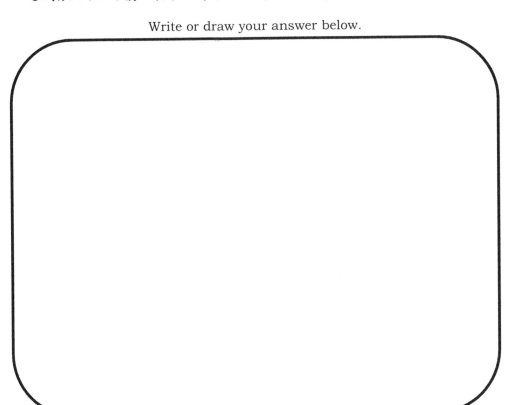

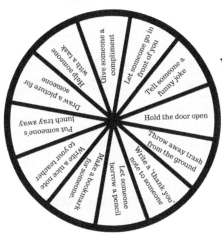

What act of Kindness did you do today? Color it in on the wheel.

Was it easy or hard?

How did it make you feel?

Day Seven

Acts of Kindness Journal

If you had ONE MILLION dollars to spend to help
someone – what you do? If you have $5 to help
someone, what would you do?

Write or draw your answer below.

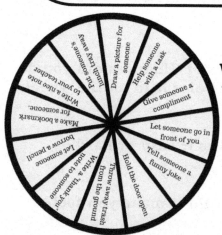

What act of Kindness did you do today? Color it in on the wheel.

Was it easy or hard?

How did it make you feel?

Day Eight

Acts of Kindness Journal

How can you help a friend when he or she is upset?

Write or draw your answer below.

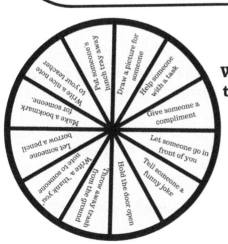

What act of Kindness did you do today? Color it in on the wheel.

Was it easy or hard?

How did it make you feel?

Day Nine

Acts of Kindness Journal

What would you do if you saw someone being picked on at the park or on a playground?

Write or draw your answer below.

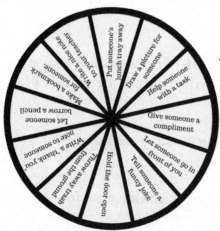

What act of Kindness did you do today? Color it in on the wheel.

Was it easy or hard?

How did it make you feel?

Day Ten
Acts of Kindness Journal
Design a "Bully Buster" Shirt to encourage "No More Bullying"

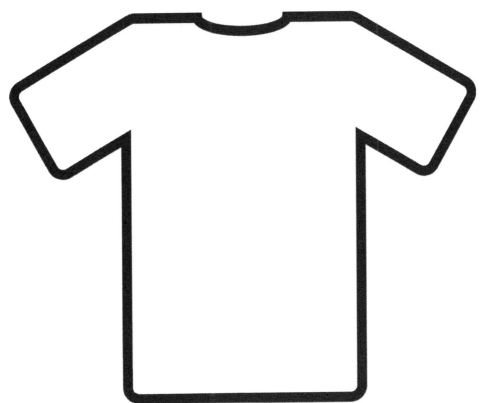

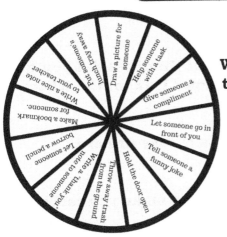

What act of Kindness did you do today? Color it in on the wheel.

Was it easy or hard?

How did it make you feel?

Day Eleven

Acts of Kindness Journal
How can you show kindness to your teacher?

Write or draw your answer below.

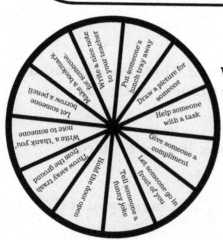

What act of Kindness did you do today? Color it in on the wheel.

Was it easy or hard?

How did it make you feel?

Day Twelve

Acts of Kindness Journal

Does someone have a task or chore that you can help with at home? Make a list of 5 things you can do.

Write or draw your answer below.

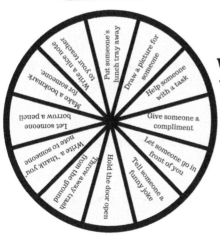

What act of Kindness did you do today? Color it in on the wheel.

Was it easy or hard?

How did it make you feel?

Day Thirteen

Acts of Kindness Journal

Describe a time that someone did something kind for you. How did it make you feel?

Write or draw your answer below.

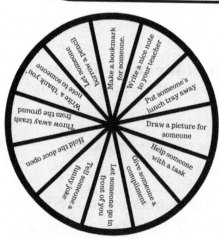

What act of Kindness did you do today? Color it in on the wheel.

Was it easy or hard?

How did it make you feel?

Day Fourteen

Acts of Kindness Journal

What is a talent, skill, or interest you have?
How can you use that to help someone else?

Write or draw your answer below.

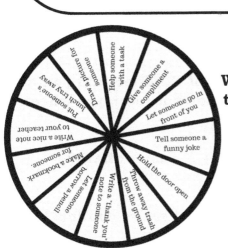

What act of Kindness did you do today? Color it in on the wheel.

Was it easy or hard?

How did it make you feel?

Day Fifteen

Acts of Kindness Journal

Would you rather... help at the animal shelter or clean up a park?

Write or draw your answer below.

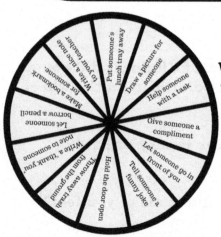

What act of Kindness did you do today? Color it in on the wheel.

Was it easy or hard?

How did it make you feel?

Day Sixteen

Acts of Kindness Journal

Would you rather... teach someone to play a musical instrument or to play a sport?

Write or draw your answer below.

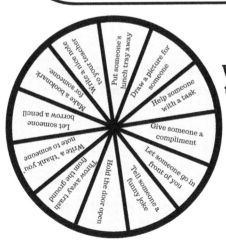

What act of Kindness did you do today? Color it in on the wheel.

Was it easy or hard?

How did it make you feel?

Acts of Kindness Journal

Design a Poster to encourage other kids to Be Kind

What act of Kindness did you do today? Color it in on the wheel.

Was it easy or hard?

How did it make you feel?

Acts of Kindness Journal

Would you rather... make a YouTube video to show kids how to Be Kind or do a skit at school? What would it be about?

Write or draw your answer below.

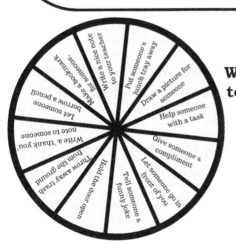

What act of Kindness did you do today? Color it in on the wheel.

Was it easy or hard?

How did it make you feel?

Day Nineteen

Acts of Kindness Journal

How can you show compassion and kindness to someone who is sick?

Write or draw your answer below.

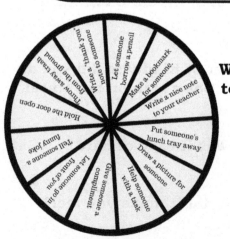

What act of Kindness did you do today? Color it in on the wheel.

Was it easy or hard?

How did it make you feel?

Day Twenty

Acts of Kindness Journal

Go back and read through your Journal. How do you feel reading what you wrote?

Write or draw your answer below.

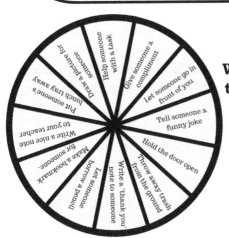

What act of Kindness did you do today? Color it in on the wheel.

Was it easy or hard?

How did it make you feel?

Acts of Kindness Journal

CONGRATULATIONS! You finished your 21 Day Journal! Celebrate by doing something kind for yourself. How can you show kindness to yourself? What do you like to do?

Write or draw your answer below.

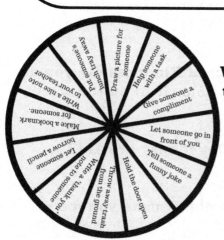

What act of Kindness did you do today? Color it in on the wheel.

Was it easy or hard?

How did it make you feel?

Project Stella Teaching Resource Center was founded by Kim David while pursuing her Master of Library and Information Science degree at Wayne State University.

The mission of Project Stella Resources is to help parents and educators find meaningful service opportunities for young volunteers to transform homes, schools, and c communities with kids who Radiate Outrageous Compassion & Kindness.

Kim David can be contacted by email at projectstellatrc@gmail.com or through Facebook @projectstellaTRC.

Learn more about Project Stella Resources and get more tips, service project guide sheets, and FREE downloads at www.projectstellaresources.com

Made in the USA
Las Vegas, NV
18 September 2021